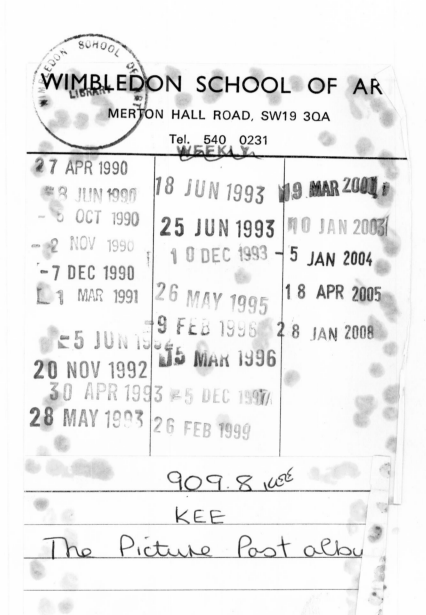

THE
PICTURE POST
ALBUM

PICTURE POST

No. 1.

October 1, 1938

80 PAGES

HULTON'S NATIONAL WEEKLY

OCTOBER 1, 1938

Vol. 1. No. 1

3D

THE
PICTURE POST
ALBUM

Robert Kee

With a Foreword by
Sir Tom Hopkinson

BARRIE & JENKINS
LONDON

First published in Great Britain in 1989 by
Barrie & Jenkins Ltd
289 Westbourne Grove, London W 11 2QA

Text © Fairrealm Ltd, 1989
Photographs © Hulton-Deutsch Collection, 1989
All pictures are the copyright of the Hulton-Deutsch Collection with the exception of
contributions from the Imperial War Museum, Popperfoto and Ullstein Bilderdienst, which are
gratefully acknowledged.

British Library Cataloguing in Publication Data

Kee, Robert, 1919-
    The Picture post album: a 50th anniversary
collection
    1. British photography, 1939-1959
    I. Title
    779'.0941

ISBN 0-7126-2058-3

Designed by Behram Kapadia
Printed and bound in Portugal by Printer Portuguesa

Foreword

by Sir Tom Hopkinson

Why do tattered copies of *Picture Post*— when any can be found — sell today for as many pounds as they once cost pence? Why do students of photography and trainee journalists write theses on a magazine which foundered long before any of them saw the light of day? Why am I, and others who were associated with *Picture Post*, continually asked whether such a magazine could succeed today, and, if so, why no-one has put it on the market?

It is a mysterious fact of life that anything which was done right, or properly constructed for its own time, often has the power to survive, even when the conditions under which it flourished have entirely changed. A flickering Chaplin comedy of silent days gives as much delight in our own all-noise, all-colour age as it did at Saturday matinées in long-vanished small-town cinemas. And a Bentley car of the nineteen-twenties, lovingly preserved, attracts fifty times the notice, and sells for a hundred times the price that it did when it first rolled out of the factory.

Such things survive today, however, as treasures for the few, not as an essential part of life. And to those who worked on *Picture Post*, the question as to whether such a magazine could achieve wide circulation and amass big profits in the altered conditions of today is beside the point. For, as Robert Kee makes clear in his admirable record of the magazine's life and premature death, we were not in it for big profits or for circulation records. Both these were necessary, and they came. But the reason why journalists, cameramen and the rest of us lived the arduous lives and worked the long hours we did, for salaries modest even at that period, was that we were determined to achieve something through the paper.

We were out to influence events in a particular direction — that of a more just and equal society. We did not think of *Picture Post* as being the property of Edward Hulton. He was the owner; he had his name on the title page, and was entitled to the profits. We didn't think of the paper as belonging to ourselves. We — the photographers, writers, editorial assistants, dark-room staff, secretaries and office boys — together created the weekly issues and felt entitled to the credit, as well as to the blame when we made a blunder.

But the magazine in reality belonged to the readers, since it existed to serve their interests. And the readers knew this. Letters did not come in to the office in handfuls, as on every other paper I have ever worked for. They came in in hundreds, and at times in sackfuls; there was a staff of four or five to see that all which required an answer got one.

So the question as to whether there can be a *Picture Post* for the nineteen-nineties breaks into two halves, and the more important half is a question which is never asked: "Would a magazine such as *Picture Post* provide an effective means for influencing public opinion on the urgent problems of today?" The answer to that must, I think, be "No". Television documentaries, radio programmes, and our few genuine newspapers reach more people, more quickly, and at lower cost.

As for the second half of the question: "Could a magazine based on still photographs and writing of high quality achieve commercial success in today's marketplace?", the answer, I have no doubt, is "Yes".

But so far it has hardly been attempted. If and when it is, the paper's aims and values are likely to be more cultural, and less social and political, than those which excited some thirty or forty young men and women, and supplied the power and driving force for *Picture Post* half a century ago.

TOM HOPKINSON

I would like to thank the following photographers, who have been kind enough to write or talk to me about the days when they worked, with such conspicuous success, for *Picture Post:* John Chillingworth, Bert Hardy, Godfrey Thurston Hopkins, Frank Pocklington, Grace Robertson, George Rodger, Humphrey Spender, Carl Sutton.

At Barrie and Jenkins, Linden Lawson, David Fordham and Bob Christie deserve a special award for patience and understanding.

My principal debt is to the efficient and industrious staff of the Hulton Picture Company and particularly to the Directors Peter Elliott and Roger Wemyss-Brooks, whose creative insight was worthy of the great days of *Picture Post* itself.

ROBERT KEE

THE PICTURE POST STORY

The story of *Picture Post* can easily be seen as a romantic one. Heralded by its first two cover girls leaping miraculously through the skies of 1 October 1938, it blazed like a comet into the world of late-thirties journalism; like a comet it travelled steadily on; and like a comet it tailed away. The same two girls re-emerged on the last cover to signal its disappearance.

The story can also be seen as a moral tale with heroes, villains and attendant princes.

But the business of everyday journalism cannot be fitted neatly into any such easy categories. It involves too much ordinary hard work, too much ultimate subjection to the press date — in the case of *Picture Post*, week after week for nearly nineteen years — too much need to compromise with inevitable commercial pressures, to be entitled to give itself lofty airs. Yet only a pedant would deny that there was something romantic about the life and death of *Picture Post* and that in its story there is, for those who wish to look for such things, a moral of a sort to be found. It is the moral which the poet W.B. Yeats once summed up to the effect that, in the business of communication, unless you please first yourself, you have little hope of pleasing anybody else.

The origins of this phenomenon in the history of British journalism are well documented. In 1934 there came to Britain as a refugee from the new Nazi regime in Germany — which had for a time imprisoned him — a brilliant and quixotic Hungarian journalist named Stefan Lorant. Lorant, who earlier in his career had been a photographer, a film cameraman and a film director, had become, before Hitler came to power, the editor of an illustrated paper in Munich, the *Münchener Illustrierte*, which, along with other German illustrated papers of the Weimar era, had developed a fresh style of picture journalism. This involved the use of a camera to unfold a journalistic story through its own eye rather than (as had been the general magazine practice until then, and still was in Britain) the publication of pictures from press and other independent sources, labelled with informative captions.

The Sorcerer's Apprentice who Became the Sorcerer himself
Tom Hopkinson, Assistant Editor 1938—40; Editor 1940—50.

The men who started it all

It so happened that Lorant's arrival in Britain coincided with the failure at Odhams Press of a paper called *Clarion*. Lorant, finding his way to Odhams, persuaded the management to switch resources into a new popular picture magazine which was then launched as *Weekly Illustrated*. Under the abbreviated title *Illustrated*, this was actually to outlive *Picture Post*, which was yet no more than a gleam in Lorant's eye. But no-one was ever to think of *Illustrated* as a phenomenon. For Lorant, whose brilliant but difficult temperament soon found itself ill at ease with an established management and with the editor they appointed, after a few months took his gleam away with him. Not, however, before something had happened which was to be crucial to the eventual phenomenal success of *Picture Post*.

Working at Odhams when Lorant went there was a twenty-nine-year-old journalist, Tom Hopkinson, an Oxford graduate

and the son of a clergyman from the clutches of whose high-minded Christian principles he had wrestled free into an enquiring manhood. The nineteen-thirties were a time when middle-class British youth, brought up in the shadow of the First World War and of society's subsequent failure to build a "land fit for heroes", was beginning to question the established order with a new individuality. Hopkinson, who had been Assistant Editor of *Clarion* and was now employed on *Weekly Illustrated* to write captions, soon realised that Lorant understood photographs in a way no-one else he had ever met understood them. He wrote later that as a result he himself came "to recognise photography as a journalistic weapon in its own right, so that if—like myself at that time — you are determined to promote causes and affect conditions, photographs can be a potent means for doing so". This is exactly how *Picture Post* was to operate.

The Gleam in the Eye from which a Phenomenon Was Born
Stefan Lorant (on the left), Editor, and Edward Hulton, Proprietor, in 1938.

A Genius with Photographs
Stefan Lorant, once Hitler's prisoner, Editor of Picture Post 1938—40.

Journalists who Used Photography as a Weapon
An early editorial conference. Left to right: John Langdon-Davies, W.H. Pearson, Lionel Birch, Richard Darwall,
Honor Balfour, H.E. Bewick, Tom Hopkinson, Stefan Lorant

Lorant, meanwhile, had borrowed money from a girlfriend to start a new-style pocket magazine called *Lilliput*, which published alert articles, sharp short stories and specialised in a formula for juxtaposing apparently unrelated photographs in such a way as to give them oblique and often humorous point (Gracie Fields next to a cathedral angel; A.P. Herbert next to a koala bear). Hopkinson continued to write captions for *Weekly Illustrated*, an exercise which in the flat context of that paper he sometimes found so boring that he began to develop his own style for livening it up. On one occasion captioning a herd of wild horses galloping free across a plain, he wrote to the effect that the horses had had enough; they were going on strike for better hours and working conditions. A postal order received by the paper the next week from an old lady making a contribution to the horses' strike fund effectively demonstrated the power which picture and caption could generate in harmony.

Lorant was successfully running *Lilliput*; Hopkinson was still at Odhams. But a third figure was about to enter the scene, as curiously different in personality from the other two as they already were from each other. This was Edward Hulton, a young Old Harrovian and Oxford man who had trained for and been called to the Bar and had stood unsuccessfully for Parliament as a Conservative candidate. Hulton's father had founded a substantial newspaper empire which included the *Evening Standard* and had sold this out in 1923 for a formidable sum which was to be inherited by his son. But the young Hulton was not allowed to enter into his inheritance until he was thirty, an age which he reached in November 1936, by which time, though he had started to practise as a barrister, he was chafing to be able to prove himself as successful as his father had been. He used his money to found a publishing company, the Hulton Press, and was already proprietor of *Farmers' Weekly* and *Nursing Mirror* when Lorant succeeded in selling to him for a sizeable sum his

pocket magazine *Lilliput*. More important: Lorant also sold him the idea for a new magazine altogether.

Hulton himself does not seem to have been clear what he was getting from Lorant with the new magazine, thinking, he admitted later, in terms of some reforming Conservative political review to give expression to the new ideas with which he, in his own fashion as a young man of the thirties, was increasingly preoccupied. What in fact he was buying was the gleam in Lorant's eye.

For with the backing of Hulton's considerable financial resources Lorant now saw himself in a position to implement in Britain those ideas of photo-journalism which had been the hallmark of the German magazines and of which Hopkinson had already glimpsed the potential. Lorant had no difficulty in persuading Hopkinson to leave Odhams to become his Assistant Editor at Hulton Press. Within less than three months of hectic, even chaotic, planning in which the title itself was until quite late uncertain (it was at one time to have been called *Lo!*), and after a lively advertising campaign and the pledging of part of Hulton's personal fortune with the bank, *Picture Post* appeared on the stands for the first time on 1 October 1938.

Something of the whirlwind character of its birth attached itself to the public perception of the event. No-one had known anything quite like it before. People found they liked what they got. In an easy way it seemed to strike a note which they had wanted struck without having previously realised it. It was indeed struck at what a sociologist has called "an extraordinary historical conjuncture". The three men concerned were each in their own way motivated by a contemporarily tuned journalistic instinct rather than specific commercial or other dogma.

This is the happiest formula for journalistic success and *Picture Post* was an immediate one.

Lorant had only guaranteed Hulton that he could sell a

The Founder who Broke Through and Faltered
Edward Hulton, the wealthy young Conservative who helped bring Labour to power but, changing his tune, was to lose his way.

What, then, was its secret? What was the public nerve with which the journalistic instinct of this hybrid trio was in touch?

quarter of a million copies but he was confident he could do better and in fact printed three-quarters of a million. Within weeks it was selling a million copies and within six months over a million and a half, with an average calculated readership of five per copy. It was to remain at that level of popularity for many years; paper shortages during and after the War alone restricted sales.

The very first issue displayed all the essential characteristics which, in often dramatically changing times, were to distinguish it for the next decade and more. The most important of these was an unassuming confidence in itself.

This first issue had actually been put to bed at the height of the Czech crisis of autumn 1938, at the moment when the British Prime Minister, Neville Chamberlain, had just heard from Hitler at Godesberg that he intended to march his armies across the Czech frontier in the immediate future, come what may. No-one then knew for certain that Britain would not, at the moment of the paper's appearance, be plunged into a world war of instant devastation and horror. With the happy cow-girls leaping across the cover, the printing presses of the Sun Engraving Company at Watford were already turning before anyone could safely predict that Chamberlain at Munich, by giving Hitler what he wanted, would save the peace — which, for the time being, he did. When, after the Munich Agreement had been signed, the first copies of

Picture Post went on sale, there was virtually no reference in its eighty-four pages to the crisis at all. It was a stroke of luck, which, in the atmosphere of relief, the new magazine's individual approach to people and events seemed somehow to have deserved and even magically to have engineered.

Typically, the one story in the first issue which had a bearing on the Munich crisis dealt with the people who in those days were allowed onto the pavement in Downing Street, not with the people inside No. 10. Excerpts from their thoughts appeared in the captions. There was even a working man who, it just so happened, had a faint look of Neville Chamberlain himself. It was the sort of formula *Picture Post* was to use on and off for the better part of its life, just as a stylish individuality in the captions and, more often than not, a quality in the text was to raise it unobtrusively above the level of more ordinary journalism. "It isn't just that they want to see the Premier," ran the Downing Street story, "their instinct draws them nearer to the heart of things." The account of a hospital operation in the same issue began, beneath a dramatic picture in the theatre itself: "A pencil with a point as fine as a cat's whisker is poised in rubber-gloved fingers. Shrewd eyes above look across inquiringly at the other white-smocked, skull-capped figure, who is holding the limp wrist. There is an answering nod . . .".

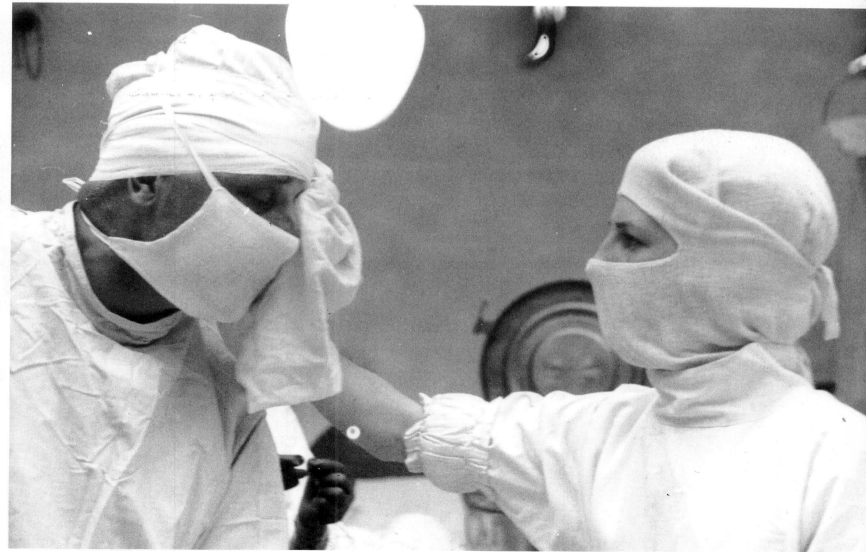

"The Human Touch"
was the caption to this picture of a surgeon and nurse in the first issue. It was printed regardless of technical blemishes,
including a hole in the top of the negative which passed for lighting.

Miner

Auction Room Blues

Trawlerman

Unemployed

A Riveter Fit for a Queen

In as much as there was to be a *Picture Post* philosophy it lay in the conviction that the lives of ordinary people, of the sort of people in fact who read the magazine, could be shown to be in themselves rewarding to curiosity, even remarkable and of worth. Life as people recognised it, and not as it passed them by, was shown as interesting. People pictured in a familiar way at their work or just standing idly by were revealed as not ordinary at all. It was not those who travelled on the transatlantic liner the *Queen Elizabeth* who counted, but the men who built her: the riveter, the boiler-maker, the engine-room worker, the joiner. Such individuals were to be photographed as if they might have been subjects for Rembrandt.

From the start, attention was to be concentrated on ordinary people . . .

... doing ordinary things ...

. . . and sometimes less ordinary things.

*"Good Wood, Madam" was the caption for the picture on the left in 1939,
while (above) "Mr Harris Finds a Fresh Deer Trail".*

The unemployed were rated to be as important . . .

...as Ministers.

Winston Churchill Roofing, 1939

Dean Acheson and Anthony Eden, 1951

Hugh Dalton and Friend, 1950

Aneurin Bevan, 1942

Lord Beaverbrook Relaxes, 1940

Clement Attlee Gets to Work, 1940

A Lecture in 1938 is a Little Too Much for Future Minister R.A. Butler

Sir Thomas Beecham, 1944

**The audience at a
Promenade Concert
were to be of equal
value with the music;**

Sir Henry Wood, 1938

Glyndebourne,
Badminton and Tattersalls . . .
were to share the spotlight with Southend.

East End Pub

The pages of Picture Post *were to be a meeting-place for people of different worlds.*

West End Café

Tyneside

Savile Row: Lionel Birch is Suited

Millionaires' Row: The French Ambassador's Wife Steps Out

Drama students were to be valued as highly as stars...

though stars were not to be neglected.

Alec Guinness, 1953

John Gielgud, 1944

Marlene Dietrich, 1944

A "glamour girl" on her day off or behind the scenes was as revealing as she was on stage – though this was no reason not to see her revealed on stage as well.

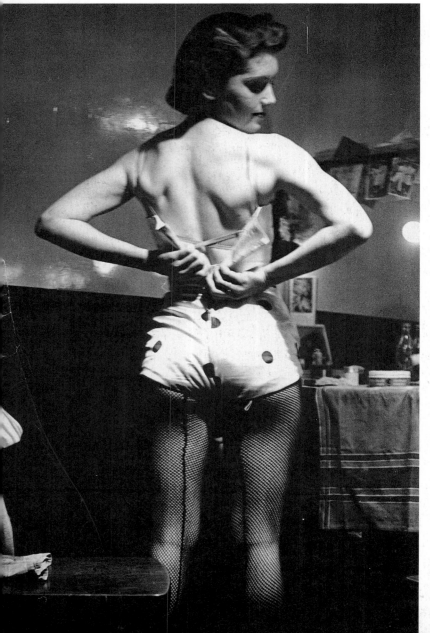

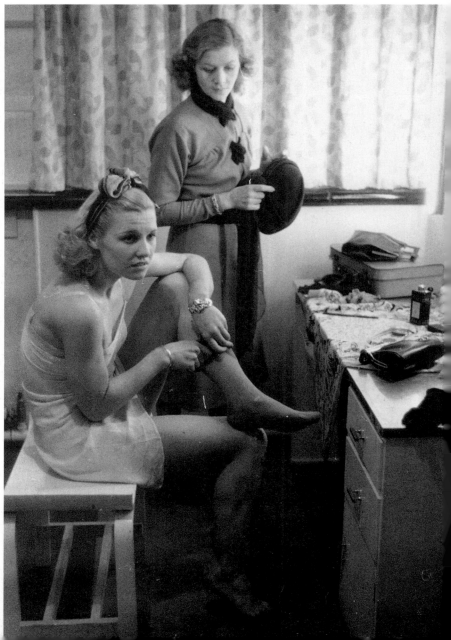

Wigan, 1939

Pimlico, 1954

The poor were to be . . .

Liverpool, 1949

The New Forest, 1949

The Lambeth Walk, 1938

...as poetic in their humanity...

Yorkshire, 1945

Wales, 1941

Gorbals, Glasgow, 1948

Liverpool, 1955

Kent, 1951

... as the poets themselves –

John Ormond Thomas, Poet and Picture Post Journalist, 1948

Laurie Lee with Roy Fuller, 1949

Rhapsody in Hyde Park, Michael Clifton, 1948

John Masefield, Laureate, 1945

Robert Graves, Bullfight, Spain, 1954

– the poets and other writers.

Dylan Thomas, 1950

Françoise Sagan, 1955

Aldous Huxley, 1948

Brendan Behan, 1956

Angus Wilson, 1952

Osbert Sitwell, 1949

Somerset Maugham, 1946

John Osborne, 1956

The sports and pastimes ...

. . . of the common man . . .

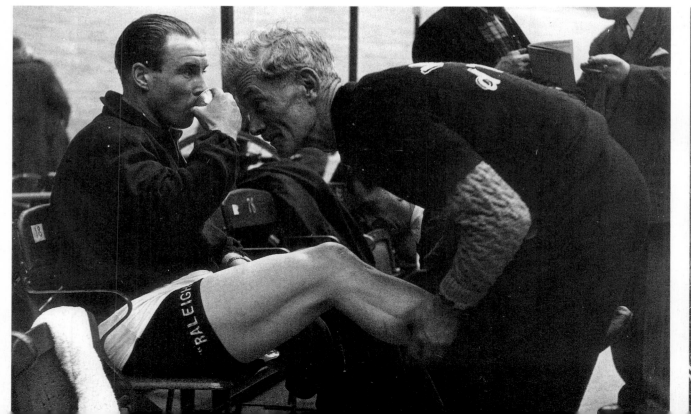

. . . were to be as interesting as the sports . . .

. . . and pastimes of the well-to-do –

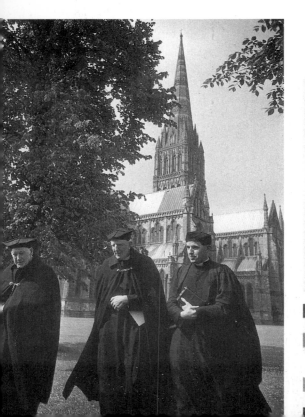

– not least when the two coincided.

Today this seems a routine enough approach. Then, as central journalistic policy, it was revolutionary, although its spirit was in fact very much in tune with one particular thirties mood. Something similar had already been in the air for a while.

Tom Hopkinson Goes In to Bat for a New Style of Journalism

In the Steps of the Film-Makers

Tom Harrisson, Founder of Mass Observation

One of many documentary film-makers of the time, John Grierson (*Granton Trawler,* 1934), defined what he and others were doing in their films as fulfilling "a desire to make a drama from the ordinary to set against the prevailing drama of the extraordinary; a desire to bring the citizen's eye in from the ends of the earth to the story, his own story of what was happening under his nose". The Old Etonian George Orwell was exploring similar social themes.

An organisation called Mass Observation had been founded in 1936 to make detailed anthropological studies of the thoughts and life-style of the ordinary citizen. Its founder, Tom Harrisson, was a friend of Tom Hopkinson, and a Mass Observation photographer, Humphrey Spender, was one of the first to work for the paper. (Humphrey Spender was a brother of the poet Stephen, whose friend W.H. Auden had written a verse commentary for Humphrey Jennings' documentary *Night Mail.*) What was original about *Picture Post* was the transfer of such interest to mass-circulation journalism. The wonder was that no-one had thought of doing it before.

Before the first year was out a popular

Sydney Kyte: Falling in Love with a Picture in Picture Post

A Trawlerman's Story

song called "Picture Girl" was recorded by Sydney Kyte and his band, with a lyric which ran:

"When I saw your picture in the
Picture Post
I fell in love with you."

It was originally the idea of a clever publicity man. In fact it conveyed in a neatly sentimental way exactly what the paper was about, and the record and the sheet music sold very nicely too.

This was all a long way from Hutton's original "political review", but he had nothing to complain about.

Even in the occasional solid pages of text there was an exhilarating freshness of tone. They held an unpatronising concern for popular education and culture, carried with an almost evangelical but undemanding air. It was not just a matter of covering stage productions, opera and film, but of dealing with a breadth of information which the man in the street might well wish to have. There were articles which brought him up to date with the findings of modern science (calories, carbon monoxide poisoning from petrol fumes, "what happens when we drink alcohol"). There was a series on great national institutions (like the RAF). There was a long-running series on great British artists, and there were short stories and other contributions by writers as varied as Stephen Leacock, Dorothy Parker, Julian Huxley, H.G. Wells, William Saroyan, Evelyn Waugh and Jane Austen. *Picture Post* was long able to carry the names of distinguished intellectuals in its pages as if, when they felt like doing so, they naturally belonged there.

"Men of the Air Reserve Run to Take Off in Defence of London
Highly efficient is the Reserve Air Force whose members, in case of war, receive immediate
commissions in the RAF. Pilots above run to take off in defence of London during air manœuvres."

A "great national institution" and some

Evelyn Waugh

Julian Huxley

H.G. Wells

Dorothy Parker

arly contributors to *Picture Post*

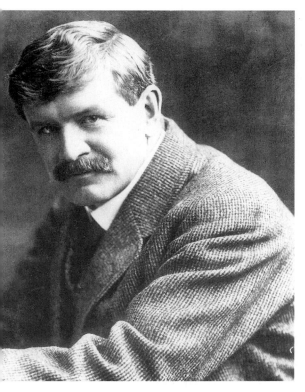

Stephen Leacock

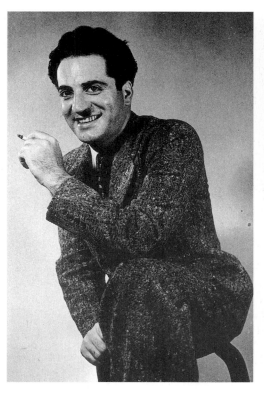

William Saroyan

Jane Austen

A certain secular earnestness in the paper may have owed something to Hopkinson's personal adjustment to the earlier clerical influence of his father; but *Picture Post* could not be accused of lacking humour or light-heartedness, or of failing to acknowledge that a bit of respectable sexiness was both agreeable and useful in helping to sell magazines.

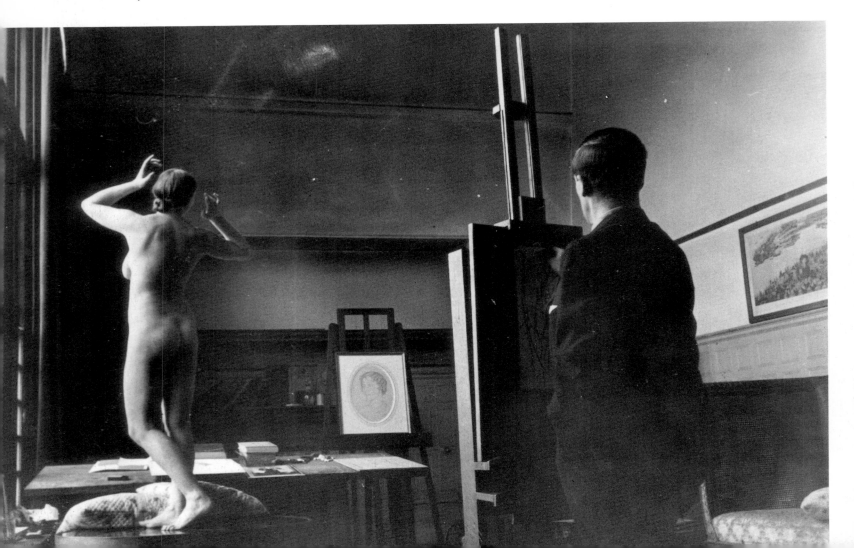

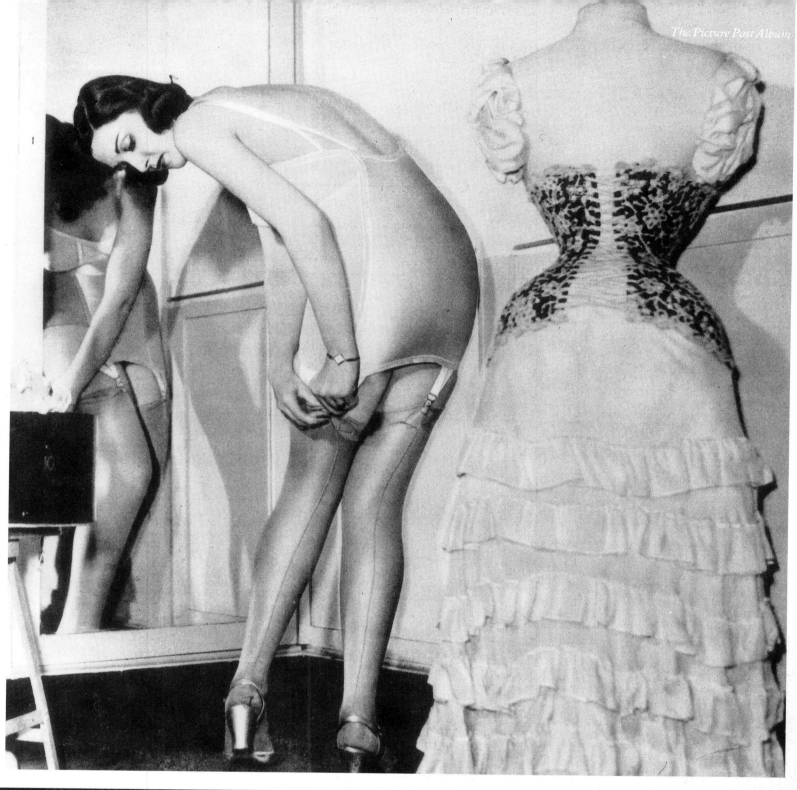

The light-hearted look

Mildly erotic pictures of showgirls and other girls cavorting in one way or another fell into occasional place without strain, while features on corsets and models were to make regular appearances throughout the years, as did artists' studios, in which a regulation nude could properly figure.

Comment on the Munich Agreement, 1938
"The elephants are happy. They are flying about the sky. [They] are happy because they have got peace. For how long have they got peace? Ah, that no-one can say."

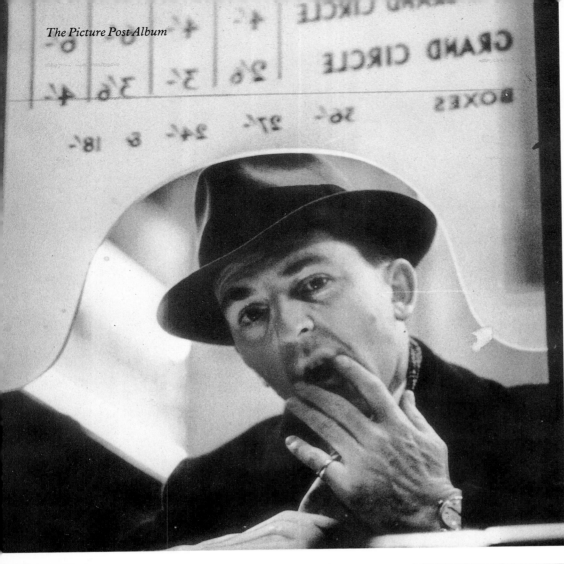

Adroit use of gentle captions constantly helped the paper sustain a good standard of undemanding picture humour.

"'No. I Think I'll Change my Mind and Have the Others'
Do women change their minds more than men? Do they forget what you said and they said, and want to begin all over again when there's a long queue behind? Do they, or don't they? These are the sort of questions no box-office manager will ever answer."

"Oh, very nice indeed, sir. An absolute corker, indeed."

"Flavour's there, right enough. But really, the colour's not quite . . ."

Cocktails for Four at a Gastronomic Festival

"Rum, very rum. Not at all sure that I like it."

"I'd not call it distinctive. Reminiscent, rather."

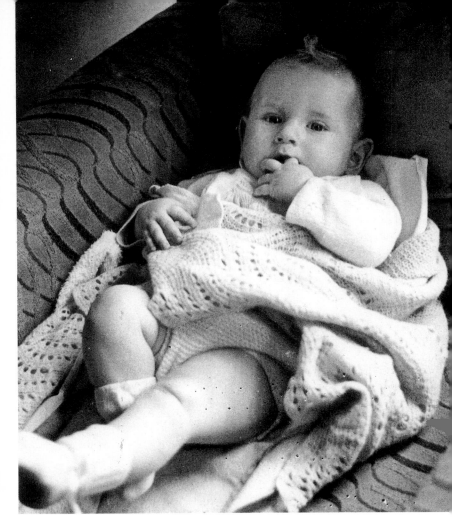

1 *"Ah! So you're the Picture Post man who's come to see what I can do. Well, get out your camera. You're going to see something very surprising."*

2 *"I stretch out the left leg to its fullest extent — about six inches. Then I tuck the right leg under it, to secure good leverage. Got that all right?"*

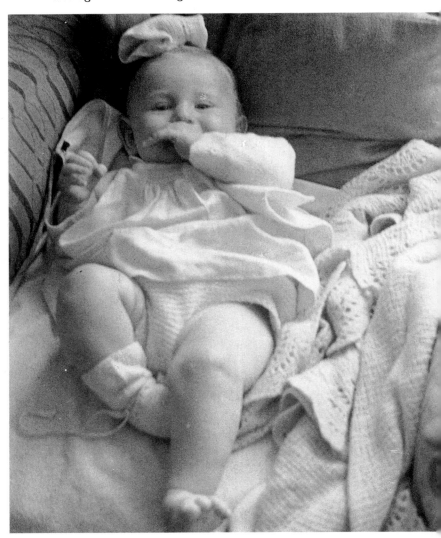

5 *". . . But I go on. I transfer the left foot from the right hand to the left, seizing hold of the left sock between thumb and forefinger of the left hand."*

6 *"Then, with a single deft twitch of the left wrist, I withdraw the sock. Place the sock on top of head, and adopt an attitude of rest."*

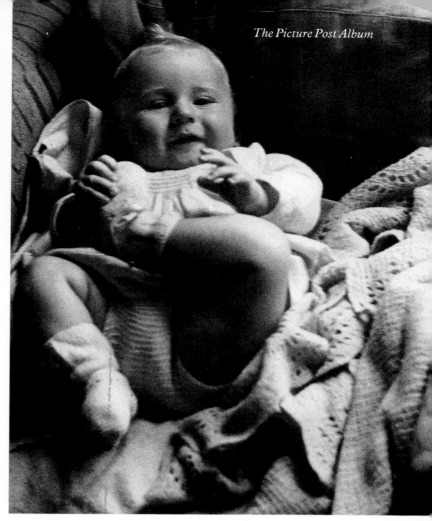

"Now I begin to draw the left leg slowly up towards the right knee. At the same time I reach slowly forward with both hands."

4 *"Ha-Ha! Done it! I grab the left foot with the right hand — falling slightly over backwards as I do so. Many performers would stop there . . ."*

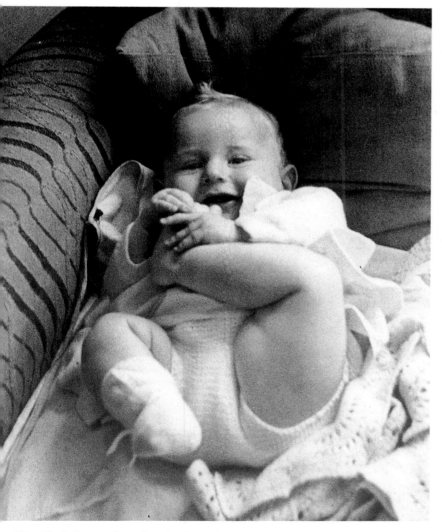

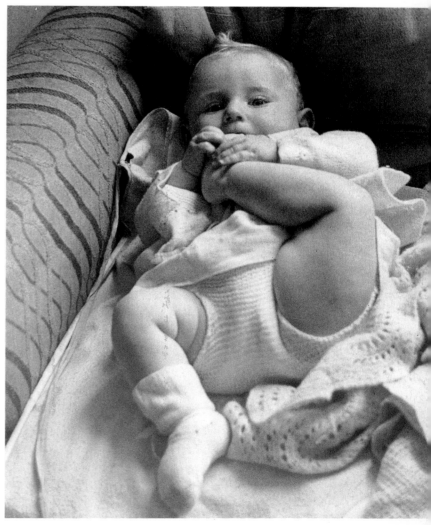

"Finally, ladies and gentlemen, to crown my amazing performance, I seize my left foot in both my hands, and draw the foot smartly up towards the mouth."

8 *"Now, to the astonishment of every onlooker, I thrust the greater part of the left foot into my mouth . . . That's all, Picture Post man. You may go."*

A bit of an elitist slip-up

The populist character of the paper emerged from its pages so effortlessly that, although it was in fact the product of middle-class idealism and a Conservative fortune, there seemed nothing patronising about its stance. Only very occasionally did a certain elitist approach unintentionally reveal itself.

A fine picture story on children going to boarding school from a railway station was introduced with the words: "First adventure, but the first parting, in the lives of most small boys, is the day when they are seen off from the station by two strangely silent partners . . ."

"*Most* small boys"? This was in no way the experience of "most" small boys, the vast majority of whom never went to boarding school at all. However, nobody, at least in the long columns of readers' letters (of which *Picture Post* at once made a lively asset), seems to have been struck by this momentarily jarring note. Indeed, there was such an unpatronising touch to the paper's populism that even now it seems unnecessarily hurtful to mention the slip. The fact that the story provided the occasion for one of Kurt Hutton's most moving pictures in any case put such fastidious criticisms out of court.

An Elite Education: The Second Stage
An undergraduate returns to Oxford, 1950.

One who's in Residence

One who's on his Way

More Figures in Elite Education: Oxford Union Debate, 1938

Oxford Dons Huddle, 1950

An Undergraduate Expands: Anthony Blond, 1950

A Future Prime Minister Holds the Floor
E.R.G. Heath (then known as Teddy Heath) speaks at the Union in 1938; the Hon. Hugh Fraser, killed in 1974 by an IRA bomb, sits at the Secretary's desk.

A Future Official of Chatham House in Waiting
Keith Kyle, later to be a journalist and to work for the Institute of International Affairs, doodles in the Secretary's chair.

But the paper's photographers at least could not help showing that while those who did not go to boarding school might be less privileged...

... they often managed to look less glum.

Hulton's imprint

Planning Britain: Hulton (centre) with Julian Huxley (on the left) and L.F. Easterbrook, 1941

Heavier were the columns of plain print.

When political issues were discussed in *Picture Post*'s pages, contributions from all the main parties were given scrupulously equal space. Nominally the paper had no overall political stance, or rather no overall national party-political stance. It was certainly anti-Nazi from the beginning and contained some effective pictorial indictments of that regime; but, perhaps because Hulton was at least theoretically still a Conservative, it refrained from any direct attack on Chamberlain's appeasement policy, even when Hitler made nonsense of this by taking the whole of Czechoslovakia.

Discussing the Future with Count Sforza, 1947

The nearest thing to a straightforward political lead was to be found in Hulton's almost weekly articles. Because, in later years, these became out of tune with the rest of the paper, and consequently seemed often irrelevant, their influence in the early years when they were wholly in harmony with it has perhaps been underestimated. Hulton's articles gave a distinct if slightly naïf political edge to the paper. They carried an almost revivalist air which demanded a new look at modern society in terms of the most basic human principles. "Man must build", Hulton wrote in the first issue, "up from the love of self, to love of family, city, province, country. From this he must learn to understand and love all his fellow men throughout the world." For the New Year in 1939 he wrote that "the future will be happier because it will be governed by ideals". He often tackled down-to-earth matters of the day such as "Why not a British film industry?", and "Are we spoiling Britain?" ("England's mountains green are the poor man's heritage.") Many of his early articles voiced aspirations for a "new age" just over the horizon.

The real political message of *Picture Post*, however, came not in a political form at all, which was why, in the climate of the time, it was to be so effective. This message was inherent in the whole style of the paper's journalistic philosophy, to which, for Lorant and Hopkinson, politics themselves were subordinate. A radical humanist approach to everything was what concerned them.

This, then, was *Picture Post* as it made journalistic history in Britain in the year before the War — the paper for the man in the street who could think of himself as more than just that.

1954: A Change of Tune

BRADBURY'S
CLARKE'S
ORANGE SQUASH
SPA THEATRE
KNIGHTS OF JOY
THE FLORAL HALL - SCARBOROUGH
ROBB WILTON
WESTERN BROTHERS
FLOTSAM
JOSEF LOCKE
PETER BROUGH
ARCHIE ANDREWS
WANDY TWOREK
RADIO REVELLERS
MAX WALL
DICK JAMES
BERYL REID
HEDLEY WARD TRIO
TED RAY
PETER SELLERS
JOAN TURNER
FISH AND CHIPS
Take Out
BAGS
1/.
OUR NOTED
CHIPS-PEAS
TEA BREAD AND BUTTER
2/6
SWEETS
Filleted Fish-Chips,
" Plaice-Chips,
Ham Salads,
Boiled Ham-Chips,
" " Fried-Egg-Chips,
Fried Egg-Chips,
Peas,
2/3
3/-
3/6
3/-
3/6
2/3
3d
All Meals
INCLUDE TEA BREAD & BUTTER.
Tea,
PEAS
3
Give
SATISFACTION GUARANTEED
Our Prices are Same all the

A paper at one with people on holiday;

The two girls sitting so naturally on the railings were from a Blackpool pier show, posing for Bert Hardy to show what he could do with a cheap camera to encourage readers. Below: Morecambe and Wise at Blackpool, 1953.

... *and at one with people at work;*

- *with people laughing . . .*

. . . with people talking . . .

walking . . .

and jiving . . .

... and with people doing some of the oddest things ... water-divining ... teaching a dog to skip.

Tattersalls, 1938

Above: Lambeth, 1938

Country House Sale, 1943

Below: Birmingham, 1954

Monty's Mother Goes Home, 1943

Picture Post *caught*

characters in a moment

of their own . . .

The Old Singer of Gower, 1949

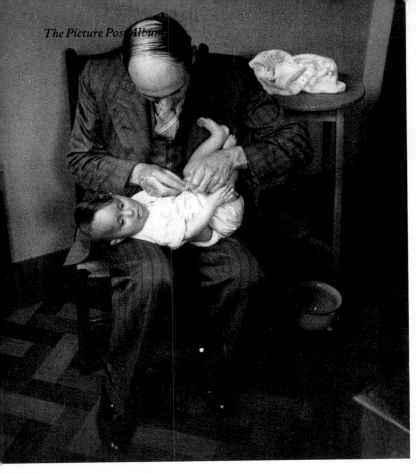

. . . without imprisoning them within it.

For all this to happen, however, the indispensable proviso was that the photography, both as executed and as laid out on the page, should be capable of making the interest interesting. Here, too, the "historical conjuncture" was both extraordinary and fortunate.

Not only did Lorant have, as Hopkinson had quickly recognised, an exceptional gift for the use of photographs and layout, but also he had available to him two exceptionally gifted photographers, both refugees from Nazi Germany, whose work with small 35mm cameras (instead of the heavy Speed Graphic and similar cameras then used by the press) was to help develop the new genre of photo-journalism in Britain. These were Kurt Hubschmann and Hans Baumann, later to anglicise their names to Kurt Hutton and Felix Man. Decisively influential as was to be their work in establishing the success of *Picture Post*— and Hutton's was to distinguish it to the very end — they would have been the first to concede that they were not, in fact, the pioneers in this field. This honour belonged to another German, Erich Salomon, a music publisher who took up photography at the age of forty-two and whose candid shots of European

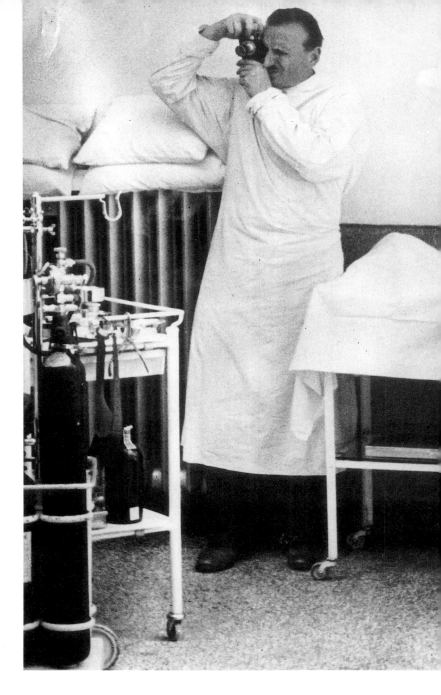

Erich Salomon

statesmen, taken with a miniature Ermanox camera, aroused fascination in the late nineteen-twenties. (He was killed by the Nazis in Auschwitz in 1944.) Nor were Hubschmann and Baumann, as is sometimes supposed, the only photographers then in Britain to have recognised the journalistic value of the small camera.

A young Londoner who had begun his professional career by collecting films from chemists, taking them to a Central Photo Service and delivering the processed prints, one day bought himself an old plate camera from a pawnshop and soon discovered, by trial and error and the application of a little practical common sense, that he had a gift for capturing both moment and feeling on film. His other hobby was cycling, and having taken pictures on club outings using this old plate camera, he found that he could sell them to a new cycling magazine called *The Bicycle*. Some of the other pictures published by this magazine struck him for their brilliant technical quality of detail, which he found himself unable to emulate. On learning that the pictures had in fact been taken by the magazine's staff photographer with a Leica, he immediately started saving money to buy one. Once he had done so he quickly began to do the staff photographer out of a job. As he later wrote: "Swinging the camera with the movement [of a bicycle race] and using it in general as an extension of my eyes came naturally to

Some early photographers

Felix Man

Kurt Hutton

Bert Hardy

me." These two simple principles, coupled with his discovery that by using forced development he could obtain pictures in almost any light, were to help make him one of the great photographers of the age. When *Picture Post*, almost at once, began to buy his pictures from the General Photographic Agency it did not even know his name. It was Bert Hardy.

The success of *Picture Post* was thus the product of a journalistic and photographic perception shared by writers and photographers. "We want what you discover, not what we tell you to discover", was the editorial brief which the photographer Humphrey Spender remembers from the early days. The same brief was given to the writers. Many years later young journalists joining *Picture Post* were always told that their first task was to learn to work with photographers, that it was journalistic vision in the pictures that made a picture story, and that words went with the pictures to enhance their effect. The dynamic thus immediately achieved by Lorant and Hopkinson and their first photographers, backed by writers like Lionel Birch, A.L.(Bert) Lloyd and Macdonald Hastings, quickly became something of a model even for the American magazine *Life*. *Life* had preceded *Picture Post* but had begun its reportage with Speed Graphic cameras and soon found that it had much to learn from *Picture Post*, both in terms of camera work and lively layouts. *Life* photographers were encouraged to study *Picture Post*'s pages.

THE WAR

But to assume that the continuity of *Picture Post*'s early success was inevitable, that the dynamic could be easily sustained, is to underestimate the nature of the paper's long achievement. Social and political climates are not constant; would the paper be able to keep up its momentum as these changed? Eleven months almost to the very day on which *Picture Post* had first hit the streets, Britain was at war. The answer to the question came immediately. *Picture Post* adapted to a quite new set of circumstances effortlessly and with instant, continuing success.

If, up to the War, the paper had had something of a bright adolescent character, in the War it developed into a responsible adult. On the one hand its formula for finding interest in the lives of ordinary people could now be transferred easily to submariners, bomber pilots, paratroopers or even the Home Guard — interspersed as before with a variety of looks behind the scenes, at opera or plays in production, at dancing girls, and at the peace of the countryside for which, somehow, it could be felt that we were now fighting. Alongside went a steady, informed analysis of the way the War was progressing.

The proprietor, Hulton, struck the paper's individual note early in the "phoney war", with an article headed "Muddle" (" . . . although we have been at war for nearly three months muddle is still enthroned . . ."). This was just the sort of responsible populism with which to confront authority.

A Scene to be Played Out Somewhere in Britain on Every Day of the War

KEEP OUT!

This is a private war. The War Office, the Admiralty, the Air Ministry and the Ministry of Information are engaged in a war against the Nazis. They are on no account to be disturbed. Nothing is to be photographed. No one is to come near.

BY ORDER

"**BLACK-OUT:** *A Symbol of the War which Mustn't Be Photographed*

We began this War with high hopes, because we felt we had a job to do. We were told that propaganda was of first-rate importance. We felt we could show the British people what their fighting forces were doing, and show the world how Britain was reacting to the War. Not at all! For a few weeks we knew there would be confusion. But now — two months after war began — we get twenty pictures showing the German side of the War for every one showing the British. Is this war? Is this democracy? Is this common sense?"

"*Some of the Leaflets our Airmen Dropped on Germany*
Our country has at least done something in propaganda. Our planes have dropped leaflets over Germany. But the leaflets are a dead secret. Only Germans may read them. Britons may not. We asked to be allowed to show them to you. Permission refused."

The absurdity of some of the early Ministry of Information censorship was exposed by the use of black blank spaces where censored photographs should have been, with the captions which would have illuminated them intact underneath, while alongside ran an uncensored photograph of the men who had ordered the censoring. When the War became more threatening in 1940, *Picture Post* took its own defence initiative and, with the technical help of men who had fought for the International Brigade in the Spanish Civil War, set up a private school for training the Home Guard, even manufacturing its own cheap but effective mortar for home use against the enemy in English villages for 38s.6d. But it was also very characteristic of a paper which had already several times mixed fascinating use of early photographs with historical information (the revolutions of 1848, the Indian Mutiny, the American Civil War) that it should, in an issue of August 1940, when the danger of German invasion was acute, have been calm enough to publish an eight-page feature entitled "How to Invade Britain". This gave an historical account of Napoleon's plans of over a hundred years before.

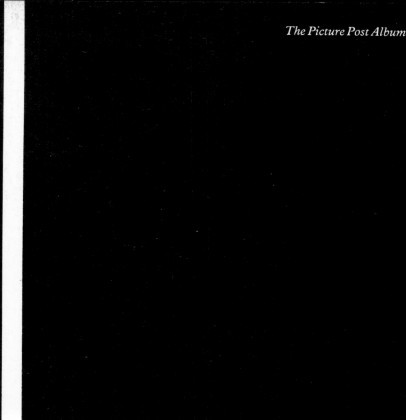

"PICTURES WE SHOULD LIKE TO PUBLISH:
British Airmen Shoot Down German Planes
A German raider crashes into a hillside — only one of dozens of pictures we should like to publish. We cannot. We can see the need of a reasonable censorship. We can't see the need of a black-out. Can you?"

"British Troops Are in Comfort in the Front Line
So well-built are the lines which British troops have occupied in France that even in recent floods they are bone-dry. You see troops enjoying lunch — or would if we were allowed to send a cameraman. Repeated requests to War Office produce nothing but courteous acknowledgments."

It was at this point in the paper's own history that the Editor, Lorant, not unreasonably decided that, with or without the British nationality he had been trying to acquire, he was, as an anti-Nazi Jew who had already escaped once from Hitler, more likely to survive somewhere else than in Britain. He sailed to America on one of the last boats on which it was possible to book a private passage.

So personally, however, had Hopkinson by this time absorbed Lorant's talent for photo-journalism that the brilliant Hungarian's departure brought about no discernible difference in the character of the paper at all. Reduced in size by the paper restrictions to a mere twenty-eight pages (it had been one hundred and four pages at one time before the War), under Hopkinson's editorship it advanced from strength to strength in both journalistic quality and importance. An increasing ability to be responsibly awkward was even honoured with some further attention from the authorities when, irritated by valid enough questioning of the effectiveness of some of the military equipment in the Middle East, the Ministry of Information tried to limit its circulation among the troops there by temporarily withdrawing the government subsidy paid to retailers. Very typically *Picture Post* turned this action itself into an important issue to be questioned.

"OUR THANKS ARE DUE TO THEM FOR THE PICTURES ON THESE PAGES:
The Picture Censorship Department of the Ministry of Information
Lord Raglan (centre) and two colleagues in the department of the Ministry of Information which decides which pictures the press may have and which it may not. Without their co-operation and far-seeing initiative, we could never have presented these exciting pictures of Britain at war."

Home defence

Army

Training for Victory

Suffering Defeat: Dunkirk, June 1940

Training for Reality: The Face of Battle

Navy

Destroyer

Submariner

Fleet Air Arm

Air Force

"We Find Them on the Uplands"

"We Find Them in the Woods"

"We Find Them in the Hop Fields"

"And We Find Them in Little Bits"

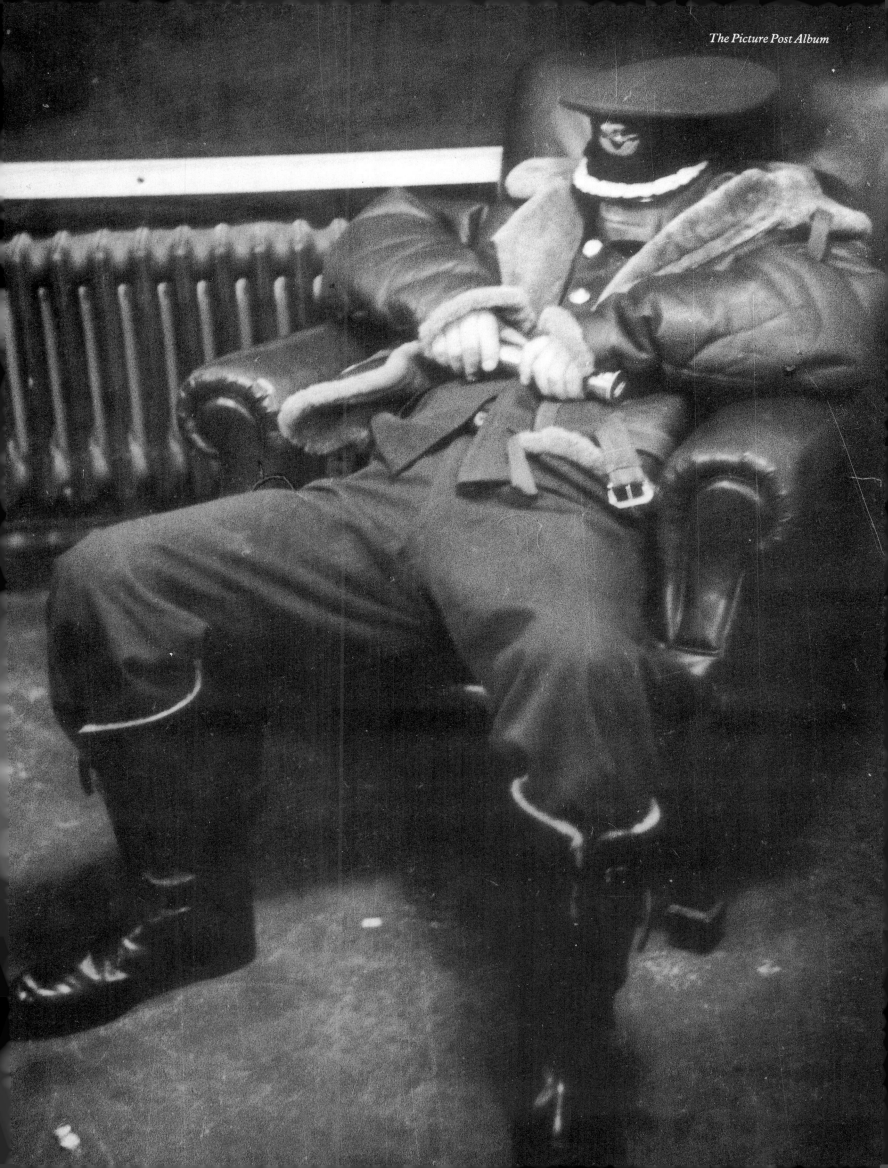

Women at war

Children at war

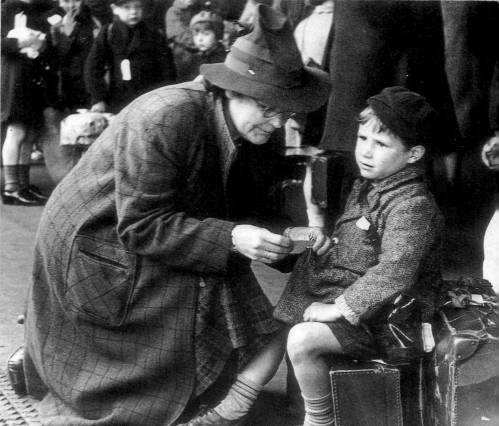

The Living Sheltering in the Underground Uncannily Suggest the Dead They May Soon Be

Men, women and children at war

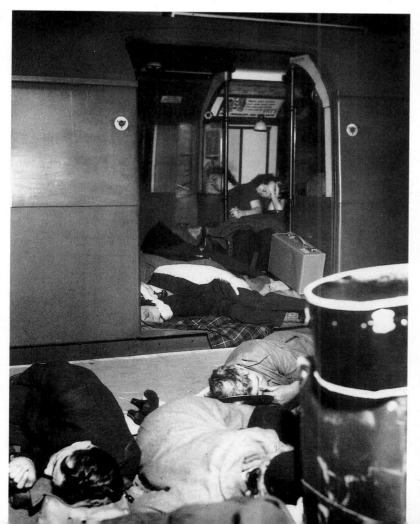

Shelter nights . . .

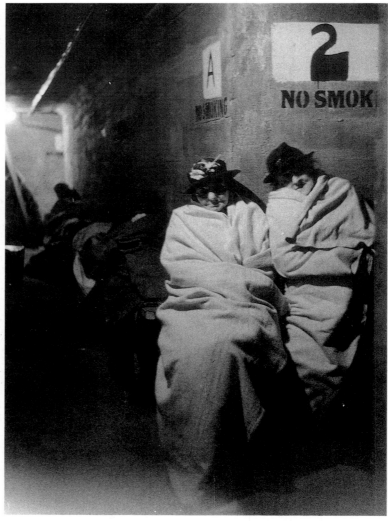

... and rubble-strewn days

The mornings after . . .

WE ARE LIVING HERE 54 LETTERS IN 52. PLEASE THANK U KIND SIR

...the nights before

And the desperate

attempt to get going again, sometimes with nowhere to go

For some there would never be anywhere to go again

The paper continued, on general themes, with what had always been one of its most effective journalistic instruments, the question mark. ("Can Bombing Beat Germany?" "What's Wrong with the Fleet Air Arm?" "What's to be Done with Germany after the War?" "The Famine in France — does it Matter to Us?") Always such questions were discussed with an air of earnest responsibility and without sensationalism. Just before the invasion of Italy in 1943 the paper had been offered an article suggesting that any such move would be a strategic error for the Allies. But Hopkinson decided not to publish it for fear of creating unnecessary alarm and despondency. Instead, to coincide with the attack on Sicily, he published an historical piece about the time when British troops last landed there, one hundred and forty years before.

Once the Italian operation had indeed become bogged down, *Picture Post* itself began to ask questions and published an article by the previously rejected author in which he scrutinised the validity of the whole campaign. Criticism was made explicit on the grounds that lessons must be learned "if final victory is to come soon".

"What's Wrong with the Fleet Air Arm?"

"What's to be Done with Germany after the War?"

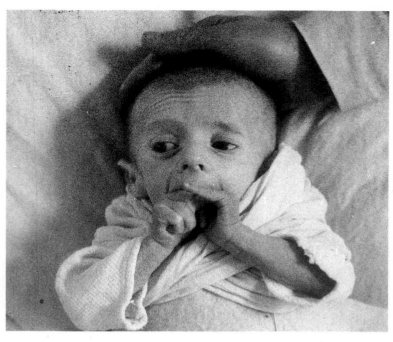

"Yes, Bombing Can Beat Germany"
Opines Air Chief Marshal Sir Arthur Harris

A Future Citizen of the
Great French Republic

Sicily: The Second Time in 140 Years

Looking for a Way Round Coupons: 1943
A Women's Voluntary Service depot, where children's clothing could
be exchanged. "When it comes to rationing," ran the original caption,
"children often get the worst of it."

A Would-be Derby Winner Tries his Paces

At the same time, during the War the paper never lost sight of a humanist approach to life in general. Quite apart from advice tendered by the Home Correspondent, Anne Scott-James, on how to make fashionable use of clothing coupons or to deal with the black-out, it was able to arouse curiosity on matters such as "Snowdonia — should we make it a national park?" This became a topic for consideration in the same issue of July 1944 which portrayed the arrival of war in a Normandy village. An earlier issue at the end of April that year had carried a red band at the bottom of the cover runnning "Last advice by military critics on the second front". The cover above it showed simply a gambolling foal whose parents, Sun Chariot and Blue Peter, had won all five classic races between them. Inside there was a five-page feature on fishing by Macdonald Hastings and Bert Hardy, who were later to cover the invasion together.

The special issue which appeared to coincide with that invasion was a typical Hopkinson product. Devoted to France, with articles by, among others, Cyril Connolly and Rebecca West, it was published both as a tribute to the courage, determination and fighting spirit of France and in order "to present some reflection of French civilisation . . . to the millions of our people who have not had the chance to make contact with this civilisation in their own lives".

A War Elsewhere: Quiet Flows the Trout Stream

WAR COMES TO NORMANDY

Two for whom it Was Soon Over
Among the first to go, they were among the first to come back, unrecognisable. Lieutenant Reeve
from Bedford; Corporal Rogers from Burnley.

Contemplating the silent revolution

A High Priest of the New Society Ponders at Bournemouth the Prospect after the War
J.B. Priestley, novelist, playwright and broadcaster. His articles and broadcasts during the War preached a benevolent populism to transform the nature of British society.

But while *Picture Post* thus always continued to assert its own special individual character, it had simultaneously been extending its influence and authority in such a way as to emerge from the War as something like the popular wing of an aspiring new establishment. Unobtrusively it had developed what amounted to a clear political approach. In the context of the War this seemed no more than a national concern for present and future, which by definition had to be taken for granted in the Government itself. In day-to-day matters, the facilities available to people who needed refuge or speedy repair of their houses were an obvious cause for anxiety. But it was in looking to the future that *Picture Post* was best able to take a political stance without obviously appearing to do so. The War itself had done much of the work. There was no need to pick up a party-political label in order to make a case for social change when the War would be over. The paper had been running articles by J.B. Priestley on "Britain's Silent Revolution". Hulton, still nominally a Conservative, had articulated as early as October 1942 what all parties were feeling, namely that the War had made one nation of Disraeli's notorious two. "This war", he wrote, "is truly welding us. We must solemnly resolve to keep up the process in the peace."

Picture Post strongly backed Sir William Beveridge's plan for social reform and was to take up a belligerent stance when it claimed to see this plan being "filleted" by the Coalition Government. A feature about what had happened after the end of the First World War concentrated on the thought: "We've got to do better this time."

With the Labour Party in the Coalition such thoughts could appear quite free from party spirit. When there were specific political issues to discuss ("Do we want more state planning?" "Should we abolish the public schools?") these were scrupulously debated by a spokesman from each side of the fence. After all, the Tory Party itself was favouring reform, as was shown in an article which featured Peter Thorneycroft and Quintin Hogg captioned respectively: "The first thing is to win the war ... " and " ... Subject to that we press for reconstruction."

Sir William Beveridge: The Welfare State on the Drawing-Board

Call-up

Menuhin

Not Exactly Clamouring for it in Birmingham Art Gallery

While the War was on,

high-minded political themes appeared among the usual skilful *Picture Post* variety of topics such as "Yehudi Menuhin rehearses", "Exmoor ponies get their call-up" and "A prebendary of Wells Cathedral takes his stall".

Hulton continued his own slightly maundering approach to reform: "Do we need beauty?... It is my humble but earnest opinion that beauty is an absolute necessity for men and for women.... The desire for beauty has receded into the subconscious of workers long submerged by evil conditions of living. But with the new age and with better material conditions, the workers will still be clamouring for beauty."

Wells Cathedral

1945: BRAVE NEW WORLD – BRITAIN

A Future Cabinet Minister Faces her Selection Committee
Barbara Castle offers herself to the Constituency Labour Party in one of the two Blackburn seats. She was to win by over eight thousand votes.

One who Was to Lose
D.H. Parkinson lost by nearly five thousand votes.

One who Was to Win in the End
Denis Healey out this time; in, 1952.

The Election on the Door-Step: A Housewife Has her Say

A feature on the first Labour Conference after the War declared openly: "A new spirit has taken hold of the Labour Party. You felt it in the first hours of the Blackpool Conference . . . ".

When, soon afterwards, the first general election for ten years took place in Britain the paper maintained its strict nominal impartiality. Equal space was allotted to the view of each party. It could, of course, be said that *Picture Post* did not need to do any electioneering because it had been doing it subtly for a number of years. Certainly, though Labour's overwhelming victory came, in *Picture Post*'s words "out of the blue", it can have been no surprise to readers when Hulton himself greeted the result with an article headed "Welcome to a New World" and expressed a sense of relief that "the form of Conservatism represented by Lord Beaverbrook and aided and abetted by Mr Churchill has been overturned". His pre-War enthusiasm for radical change did not seem to be waning.

1945: BRAVE NEW WORLD – EUROPE

Picture Post's character had been largely formed by seeing out the old world. What was its character to be in the new one?

There were certainly serious enough matters to discuss: man's entry into the atomic age, the problem of Europe's displaced persons, of the innocent casualties of war, the new "Cold War", Palestine and China.

Abroad the paper saw few immediate grounds for optimism. At home, as a guardian of social principles which it had long fostered, it was not prepared to toady to anyone, not even to the new Labour Government.

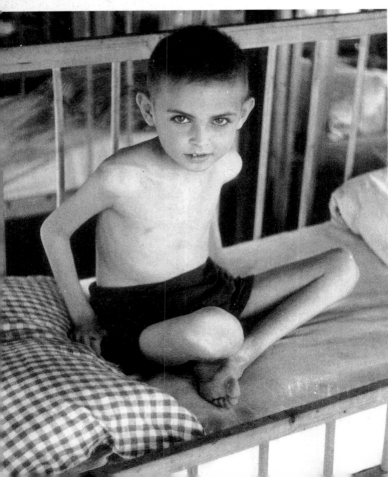

A German Boy Offers his Father's Iron Cross for Food

Men of the new Labour Government

At home, an economic crisis in Britain cast early shadows over the Labour Government.

When, in May 1947, the paper published a picture of crowds two years before, celebrating VE Day in London, the caption ran: "The day we thought our troubles were over!" It continued: "What has gone wrong?"

Left: Clement Attlee, Prime Minister
Below: Aneurin Bevan, Minister of Health

Herbert Morrison, Lord President of the Council and Leader of the House of Commons

Ernest Bevin, Foreign Secretary

"Men and Machines Fight Nature to Make New Farmlands out of Useless Bush
Not very long ago the Africans driving these great bulldozing tractors knew nothing but the simplest tools. Today in
Tanganyika's great Southern Province they pile felled trees for burning — second stage in the mechanical clearing of bush for
the production of crops to yield oils and fats."

"The African's Ambition — Choking Hours on a Bucking Giant, Mauling the Stubborn Earth
Anywhere on the bared soil, movement means dust. This tractor, pulling a ripper to loosen Kongwa's hard-compacted soil,
goes ahead of excavators levelling the site for a repair shop — an illustration of the untested soil difficulties that have eaten
money, wrecked machines and ruined easy hopes."

Fyfe Robertson at Work

There were the continual non-political

problems of life too: soil erosion, paraplegics, polio, the tsetse fly, water pollution and other such preoccupying themes for which Hopkinson produced, from one of the administrative departments of the office where the man had not been a conspicuous success, one of the most conscientious journalists ever to write for the paper. He was Fyfe Robertson, a writer capable of giving lyrical perception even to the weightiest theme. Confronting a tsetse fly, he was to find himself "seized with a ridiculous respect, a legitimate awe. For there was the real ruler of tropical Africa. More than wars, or governments, or missionary zeal, this disease-bearing insect has shaped the development of a continent . . .".

Robertson could turn his hand with equal responsibility to matters which carried a political edge. Working with the staff photographer Raymond Kleboe, he made a devastating analysis of shortcomings in the Labour Government's East African Ground Nuts Scheme, which strengthened criticism in Parliament. Parliament also paid attention to *Picture Post* after the paper had discovered that a member of the new East German diplomatic representation destined for London was an admirer of Hitler whose treatment of the Jews he thought would be brought "into perspective in fifty years time". The man did not come after all.

"Writing Reminders of a Danger Yet to be Met
On the new man-made plains, dust-devils grow and die in the heat of the day. Water-erosion is the greater danger, but heavy cropping and long bare seasons may yet show wind to be a more formidable problem than confident scientists at present believe."

"Steel Not Good Enough for the Job
Specially designed root-rakes lasted sometimes for less than an hour. And if the blades held out, dust ruined unprotected brass bushes."

The light-hearted streak

Left: Diana Dors, 1950

Opposite, bottom left: Christine Norden, 1948

Eleanor Powell

Danny Kaye

Under the quiet inspiration of Hopkinson's leadership it had always been the strength of the paper that it could leaven earnest concern with a light-hearted streak without in any way diminishing the concern. Penguins, pandas, dancers, starlets – who sometimes rose even to the cover, only to sink without trace – had always managed to remain in harmony with the rest of the paper, and continued to do so. Such things reflected the paper's own enjoyment as much as that of the people who bought it.

A Confrontation that Spelt the Beginning of the End

Tom Hopkinson, Editor since 1940, unable to accept an editorial decision of the proprietor,
Edward Hulton, was sacked. The effect, imperceptible at first, gradually made itself felt.

This harmony of often widely different items owed much to a certain touch of class in the caption writing. Hopkinson's principle that captions must enhance the picture and not just describe it had always been an essential part of *Picture Post*'s character. The touch did not have to be intrusive. The caption to an agency picture of some happy Easter chicks in April 1947 ran: "The Easter symbol of hope after Europe's worst winter since the Middle Ages." Another undemanding agency picture carried the simple narrative: "The first course in a chameleon's breakfast and the last second in a grasshopper's life." Regular coverage of the arts, particularly plays, films and opera, emphasised a sense of balance. Above all the paper had that

1950: WAR IN KOREA

supreme journalistic asset: the character of an old friend whose behaviour was nevertheless unpredictable.

Of course there were dull issues now and again, as there had always been, and issues in which the character seemed like a formula. There were also occasional mistakes. A picture feature in 1947 suggesting some analogy between Hitler and de Gaulle now seems unfortunate; the heading to a good series on Burma, Indonesia and Malaya — "Stalin's Front Line"— is also in retrospect unsubtle. (The latter trip incidentally was one of the very few in the history of the paper on which, at least in the view of the photographer Bert Hardy, relations between himself and the journalist — Woodrow Wyatt — were not as harmonious as they might have been.)

Possibly Hopkinson's greatest single mistake was when he took the decision to devote almost an entire issue to a matter which had been intriguing Fyfe Robertson for years: the claim by a Welsh healer named Rees-Evans to have achieved success in certain cases of cancer with herbal remedies. For the only time in its history *Picture Post* appeared with an array of text rather than a picture on its cover, while the introduction to the feature inside stated — inaccurately as it turned out — that advertising had been removed from the issue to signal the paper's wish not to be accused of gaining from sensationalism. The whole feature was indeed intelligently and responsibly presented and the Minister of Health of the day, Aneurin Bevan, appointed a committee composed of the President of the Royal Society, the Chairman of the Standing Advisory Committee on Cancer and Sir Alexander Fleming, the discoverer of penicillin, to investigate the claims.

This in itself was a tribute to *Picture Post*'s authority.

Perhaps it was as well that the committee's conclusion — that the claims did not merit further investigation — was not published until eighteen months later. But by then a far more grievous blow had been struck at the paper's authority. Tom Hopkinson had been sacked from the editorship. This had nothing whatever to do with the cancer story.

It had gradually become apparent in the period of *Picture Post*'s consolidation after the War that the proprietor, Edward Hulton, was drifting away from the direction in which the rest of the paper moved so successfully. Mostly this was apparent only behind the scenes, where Hulton, a devotee of London clubs (he belonged to six) in which the progressive slant of his paper would have been viewed askance by many members, complained to Hopkinson from time to time about the tone of some of the articles. These included reports by Sydney Jacobson and Bert Hardy on Poland where, despite Communist domination, they found a praiseworthy spirit of reconstruction. Hulton's own earlier radical tendencies — he had at one time advocated a maximum income for the rich — dwindled in the context of the Cold War which, he felt, should become the principal concern of *Picture Post*. The paper had always been one in which political attitudes were not assertive. Indeed, just because of this, when Hulton himself had an article in the summer of 1948 headed "Why I Am Not Supporting Labour", it seemed merely out of keeping with the paper's character. But the difficulties which Hopinson was experiencing with him came out into the open in the autumn of 1950.

American Troops Come Ashore at Inchon
When used in Picture Post this photograph of Hardy's was joined up with a similar one taken
by him a few seconds later to give a more coherent dramatic effect.

The Men whose Work Was Too Good for the Proprietor
James Cameron — who wrote — and Bert Hardy — who photographed — the story which
Edward Hulton was determined to ban.

In July Hopkinson had sent Haywood Magee and the reporter Stefan Szimanski (Stephen Simmons) to cover the war in Korea. But Szimanski was killed in an air crash and Magee returned to London. Now Hopkinson sent James Cameron and Bert Hardy to replace them. They sent back a number of compelling stories which appeared in the paper, including one with powerful coverage of the American landing at Inchon. Their final story was a shocking one.

The Everyday Human Face of War
Koreans, liberated twice within three months, run towards the future as if they were running away from it.
Hardy thinks this is one of the best pictures he ever took.

A Picture Hulton Had Already Published
Koreans going to their execution, photographed by Haywood Magee and used in Picture Post *in July 1950.*

The story was about the brutal treatment of political prisoners by the South Korean regime which the United Nations were supporting. Hopkinson realised at once that it was dynamite, particularly in the context of his prevailing relationship with the proprietor. He waited until Cameron and Hardy returned to confirm its authenticity and that it was no isolated case. He set Cameron to work on the story to remove any trace of excessive emotion which might lead people to accuse the paper of sensationalism or political bias. Cameron later said of the article as he finally wrote it that he had "never worked so hard to write so badly". Cameron in fact never wrote badly. He simply wrote this story in a flatter and more considered style than he would have wished to do. Hopkinson meanwhile, bending over backwards to achieve balance, found in a Czech magazine a picture of an American prisoner being paraded cruelly through the streets of the North Korean capital. He laid this out with the rest of the story and, after Hulton had been shown a copy and apparently made no objection, sent it to press.

Then Hulton, a man known to be much under the not inconsiderable influence of his beautiful wife Nika, ruled that the story should come out of the paper after all. As the man who provided the finance for the paper, he felt he had not only the right but also a moral obligation to see that material which he thought ought not to go into it should be kept out. Hopkinson agreed to take it out for a week, during which further discussion could take place, but when this led to nothing he refused to accept the management's invitation to him to resign and they sacked him. He persuaded most of the staff not to resign in protest, though A. L. Lloyd, Lionel Birch and the Fashion Editor Marjorie Beckett decided to go.

Some of the pictures Hulton banned in October 1950

Ted Castle, who Succeeded Hopkinson for Six Months

After Hopkinson; no immediate change

There was of course no immediate effect on the paper. What Hopkinson had built up was too strong for that. He secured agreement from the management that his long-standing Assistant Editor, Ted Castle, should be allowed to succeed him for a minimum of six months, and the only discernible change at first was the appearance of Castle's name instead of Hopkinson's on the mast-head. But just as many natural cataclysms have been long prepared underground, so what eventually happened to *Picture Post* had its origin in the dismissal of Hopkinson.

Even after the management had failed to renew Castle's contract at the end of six months (disliking his close connection with the Labour Party) and had replaced him with an able man from advertising, Frank Dowling, there were few observable symptoms of decline at first. Only a couple of months into his regime one of Bert Hardy's pictures of the maltreated South Korean prisoners actually appeared in the paper in an article by James Cameron on the first twelve months of the War; it was accompanied by the picture of the humiliated American prisoner which Hopkinson had intended to place in the story. Of course the very fact that it was obviously now considered uncontroversial enough to be printed, itself signalled a depreciation of the paper's journalistic values.

*Frank Dowling, who Succeeded Castle and
Was in Turn Superseded*

But it was not yet obviously a depreciation that was spreading. Possibly there began to be rather a lot of girls in the paper. But then there had always been quite a lot of girls in the paper. Possibly rather more of them were rather more undressed than before; possibly there was a little more frivolity all round than before; but then these penguins, a year after he had left, were creatures of which Hopkinson himself had always been fond. And no-one could say that the old seriousness was not there too.

A thoroughly responsible series called "Sex and the Citizen" appeared over a number of weeks, edited by Fyfe Robertson. ("The Bread Racket" and "Where are the Downland Sheep?" were to be further targets for his robustly compelling zeal.) The *Guardian* theatre critic, Philip Hope-Wallace, wrote, with certain reservations, about a new young actor, Richard Burton, playing Henry V at Stratford. A.L. Rowse wrote about England's queens when Elizabeth II ascended the throne and Sacheverell Sitwell contributed four articles on the life and death of George VI. Excellent younger writers started working for the paper: Kenneth Allsop, Jenny Nicholson, Brian Dowling (the Editor's son), Trevor Philpot and Gordon Watkins, to be joined by Robert Muller, Cynthia Judah and Gavin Lyall. Macdonald Hastings and Hilde Marchant continued to contribute as they had done since the earliest days. Denzil Bachelor continued lively sports coverage which, in the best *Picture Post* tradition, was as much about life as about sport. A well-informed Foreign Editor, Sylvain Mangeot, joined the paper. Hulton himself was sometimes found pontificating in the slightly eccentric manner of his early style, though with a different political orientation.

The price of the paper, which had at one time risen to 6d., was lowered again in August 1952 to 4d., a considerable achievement unless regarded as an indication of a need to consider, above all, the cheaper end of the market. But the appearance, in the same cheaper issue, of a feature by the intellectual Geoffrey Grigson on Wiltshire, with Hopkinson's old photographer from Mass Observation days, Humphrey Spender, seemed to belie this inference.

Nearly all the photographers who had given the paper its great name still continued to work for it: Hardy, Kurt Hutton, Haywood Magee, who had come with Hopkinson from *Illustrated* at the start, Grace Robertson (daughter of Fyfe), Charles ("Slim") Hewitt, Godfrey Thurston Hopkins, Carl Sutton, who invented an "action sequence camera" mounted on a rifle butt and able to shoot fifteen pictures per second. These were joined by younger men, talented in the same tradition, two of whom, John Chillingworth and Frank Pocklington, had worked their way up from the *Picture Post* dark-room, where wonders had so often been and were still being performed under the presiding genius of Edith Kay.

The traditional high quality of the paper's layout, originally established by Lorant, had been consistently maintained under different art editors — Edgar Ainsworth, Harry Deverson, Michael Middleton and Henry Fuller — and also long seemed to survive the departure of Hopkinson. Indeed, there were times when one could hardly believe that his touch was not still around. A feature in the issue dated 15 October 1952 about the English autumn by Macdonald Hastings hit exactly the note of stylish charm which had distinguished the paper in the old days. "The biggest news of the week", ran its introductory matter, "is printed in small type, almost apologetically, at the top of the page [where the date was]. It's October." Lionel Birch, who, with Hastings, had been in Lorant's day one of the paper's first reporters, was back with it again by the end of that year, before long to succeed Dowling as "Executive Editor". Only imperceptibly was there something wrong.

The trouble with the imperceptible is that it becomes perceptible in the end. In the same month as the October feature there appeared in *Picture Post* a Horlicks advertisement set out exactly like a double-page *Picture Post* article. "Conquest of Stress and Strain", it was headed, "by V.H.Mottram M.A., late Professor of Psychology in the University of London"; and to one side was a good *Picture Post*-type picture of a girl relaxing. It was almost as if it had been commissioned under the benevolent eye of Fyfe Robertson. It was an early straw in the wind: the management was relying on the selling of advertising to keep the paper afloat rather than on the character and content of the paper to sell the advertising. A year later a special feature on "Heat and Light in Your Home" with "Ten pages of practical suggestions for maintaining your home brighter and warmer this winter" appeared surrounded by ten pages of advertisements for the very things that might help you to do so and the shops where you could buy them. At the same time the continually extended use of colour somehow gave the impression that the paper was striving for popularity whereas in Hopkinson's time the popular features had not done that. The now regular monotony of a pretty girl on the cover was too often duplicated by a double-page centre spread of the same girl in colour showing rather more of herself than on the cover.

None of this in theory interfered with the talent that continued to be displayed in text and pictures. But inevitably it suggested that the talent was no longer the paper's only asset, as had

And some of the people who throughout the life of *Picture Post* were to be found within it at different stages of theirs

Opposite page, clockwise from top left:
Benny Hill, 1955; Louis Armstrong, 1956;
Elizabeth Taylor, 1952; Brendan Behan (on
the right) and Lucian Freud, 1952

This page: (right) Frank Sinatra, 1953;
(below) the royal family, 1947

Benjamin Britten (second from right), with Peter Pears (on the left) and E.M. Forster (second from left), 1949

Bob Hope, 1945

George Formby, 1943

Jacob Epstein, 1939

Lady Bonham-Carter with Tom Driberg, 1956

Frankie Laine, 1954

Dimitri Shepilov, 1956

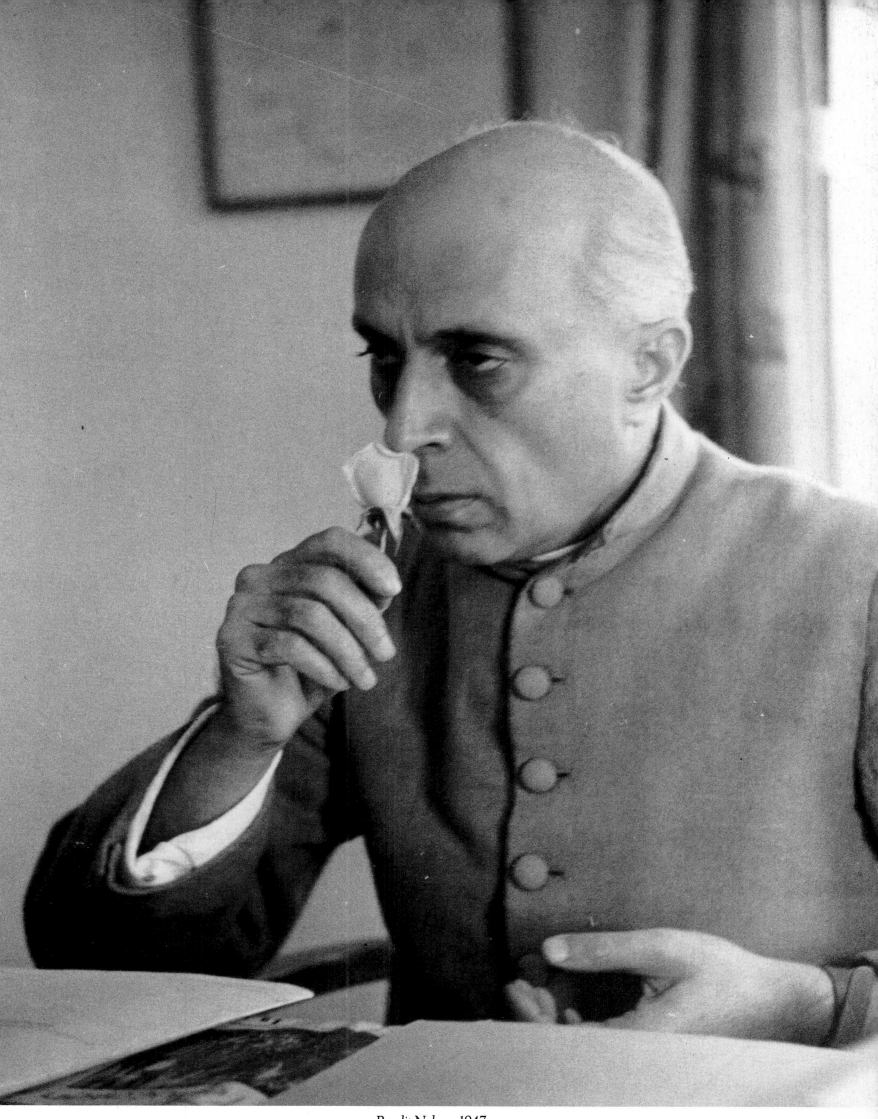

Pandit Nehru, 1947

Margot Fonteyn, 1946

Glen Miller, 1944

George Bernard Shaw, 1939

Clockwise, from above: Michael Foot, 1945; Salvador Dali, 1955;
King George VI, 1944; Osbert Lancaster, 1944

This page:(top) Richard Dimbleby, 1953; (left) Bertrand Russell, 1945

Opposite page:(top) Brigitte Bardot, 1956; (bottom left) Harold Macmillan, 1948; (bottom right) Eva Peron, 1950

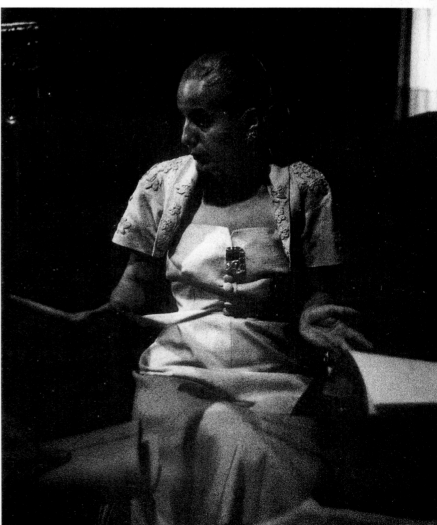

This page: (above) David Ben Gurion, 1946; (below left) Queen Elizabeth with Queen Marie of Yugoslavia, 1943;(below right) Gregory Peck, 1953

Opposite page, clockwise from top left: Amaryllis Fleming, 1953; John Maynard Keynes, 1940; John Gielgud, 1943; Tommy Trinder, 1943

Opposite page: (top) Augustus John, 1941; (bottom left) Jean Cocteau, 1956; (bottom right) Robert Graves, 1941

This page: (above) Richard Burton, 1951; (below) Jomo Kenyatta, 1945; (right) Emlyn Williams, 1940

Gilbert Harding, 1953

Lloyd George, 1940

Ingrid Bergman with Alfred Hitchcock, 1948

T.S. Eliot, 1942

Gladys Cooper, 1948

John Huston, 1951

Opposite page: (top) Stanley Spencer with Jill Craigie, 1943; (bottom left) Lord Beaverbrook, 1949; (bottom right) Max Beerbohm, 1943

This page: (above) Ralph Vaughan Williams, 1951; (below left) Marshal Tito, 1953; (below) Richard Attenborough, 1943

Finis